SABER SAMURAI

How To Use Light Sabers To Start A
Profitable Career...

While Also Making A Positive Impact
Within Your Community.

- Sifu Armstrong

DEDICATION

Through all of my personal battles and "Mission Impossible" adventures there is a Secret Weapon that I must acknowledge and offer my Deepest Gratitude. To Sifu Julliana Armstrong, my beautiful, loving and selfless wife. Thank you for all that you do both seen and unseen by the eyes of man.

Also, to my Mother and Daughter I offer my appreciation and love. Both of you have offered many windows of opportunity for me to search within myself and discover the "Better Me" that has always been there waiting patiently for his day to shine.

TABLE OF CONTENT

CHAPTER 1:

SABERATION: Founding Masters, Influences And Origins:

Welcome! Congratulations on your decision to dive into the realm of the Saber Samurai. This manual will provide you with the historical, future and current simple steps required to increase your income and positively influence your community... all while using the Light Saber. Indeed I am so grateful and honored to live a life that I love. I have the best career on the planet, hands down, no questions asked. Not only do I actually earn a lucrative living, using Light Sabers, I help to establish positive influences within other people's lives. It is the most rewarding and purposeful experience in the world. There are literally no words that can do justice towards explaining this humbling experience. After living "The Saber Life" for several years, I've come to realize that there are very specific ways in which to have a successful and profitable career as a Saber Samurai. Being a Saber Samurai means to commit oneself to a lifestyle which utilizes the Light Saber in ways that consistently enhances other people's lives as well as their own.

Greetings. I am Sifu Armstrong. Founder of Saberation Inc., The world's first Light Saber Martial Art, Fitness and Athletic Association. Our flagship service, Light Sword Martial Arts, is a fully accredited light sword martial arts academy by means of our "Sijo" Nathan Young (Founder of the Jeet Kune Do Wing Chun Academy) under the umbrella of the American Jujitsu Institute (AJI).

The AJI is headquartered in Honolulu, Hawaii and is a Non-Profit, 501(c)(3) Educational Institution which perpetuates the teachings of Henry S. Okazaki and Kodenkan/Danzan Ryu Jujitsu. The founder of Kodenkan/Danzan Ryu Jujitsu, Henry Seishiro Okazaki, was instrumental in the formation of the AJI in 1939 when the AJI was formed and continued through the development of an official charter in 1947, which remains as the primary focus to this very day.

Saberation Light Sword Martial Arts has four Founding Masters. Sijo Nathan Young, Sifu Julliana Armstrong, Sifu Nick Benseman and myself, Sifu Edward Armstrong.

Sijo - Nathan Young is a Second Generation Instructor in Jeet Kune Do under Richard Bustillo and was awarded Grand Champion In Forms at Professor Godin's Kenpo Tournament. Sijo Young was also awarded 3rd place at the World Championships in New Orleans in 2001. In 2002, Sijo was awarded 1st place in the World Cup and invited to perform at the 2004 Olympics. Sijo Young is also a two time World Champion in the 2017 & 2019 World All Styles Championship in multiple forms.

Sijo's Nathan Young experiences and studies include graduating from the UNIVERSITY OF HAWAII AT MANOA – Honolulu, HI in 2019 where he received his BS Degree in Kinesiology and Rehab Science.

Additional Certifications, Rankings and Accomplishments include:

- Keichu-Do Karate and Jiu-Jitsu Instructor under Victor Marx, Rachael Yasui
- Brazilian Jiu-Jitsu Purple Belt under UFC fighter Joe Moreira

- APK Certified Level 2 Parkour Instructor under Travis Graves
- Elite Training Systems Instructor under Professor Kai Li
- Certified Jeet Kune Do Instructor under Richard Bustillo of IMB Academy
- Certified Jeet Kune Do Instructor under Larry Hartsell
- JKD Training with Taky Kimura, Andy Kimura, Dan Inosanto, Tim Tacket and Dr. Zee Lo
- Certified Wing Chun Instructor under Professor Kai Li
- American Jiu-jitsu Institute 2nd degree Black Belt
- 2nd Degree Blackbelt in Hapkido Under Dojunim Ji Han Jae and KHF President Oh Se Lim
- 2nd Degree Kenpo and Kajukempo blackbelt
- Certified LudoSport Form I & II Tecnico
- Bagua and Ninjutsu experience under Ray Carbullido
- Judo experience under Nathan Hiraoka
- Hawaiian Lua under Professor Olohe Dennis Eli and Olohe Kainoa Li
- Tae Kwon Do Experience under Joey Lee
- Muay Thai experience under Dan Kaetsu
- Hung Gar, Lua Gar, Mantis, Drunken Fist under Daniel Lau
- Wushu under Guoxing Liao and Master Jing Li
- Aikido Experience under William Hufen
- Capoeira Experience under Victor Hwang

Sifu Julliana's Martial Arts accomplishments include being awarded 1st Place in the 2019 Global Stick and Blade Alliance (GSBA) Eastern Region Tournament for both Women's Mixed Weapons Division And Women's Single Padded Division. Sifu Julliana continued on towards being awarded 1st Place in the 2019 Global Stick and Blade Alliance (GSBA) National Championship for Team Carenza Performance under the leadership and guidance of Master Glen Spence from Applied Martial Arts Academy. Sifu Julliana Armstrong is also certified through the National Academy Of Sports Medicine (NASM) as a Personal Fitness Trainer.

Throughout her Saber Samurai journey, Sifu Julliana became the first Primary Light Saber Sport and Dueling Instructor contracted by Langley Air Force Base and Fort Eustis Army Base as well as the First Certified Instructor for Officials of an International Light Saber Combat Franchise. (LudoSport International) Light Saber Combat (INCOM). Allowing her to become the First American to ever referee the Annual International Light Saber Champion's Arena held in Milan, Italy.

After owning and operating her own bilingual Tax and Insurance Agency servicing several thousand clients for nearly a decade, Sifu Julliana accumulated over 30 years of experience in the customer service industry and has helped organize, run and grow several businesses across various industries. Sifu Julliana has also been the key person and primary organizer for over a dozen successful public events and workshops.

Sifu Nick Benseman grew up within the film industry of Los Angeles, California and found his love of movies and martial arts. Sifu Nick started at a young age studying the disciplines of martial arts. His studies include:

- Jun Fan Gung Fu,
- Jeet Kune Do -
- Dan Junod a private student of both Sifu Ted Wong and Sifu Jerry Poteet (Bruce Lee's philosophy),
- Wing Chun,
- Tae Kwon Do,
- Danzan-Ryū JuJutsu,
- Judo,
- Kenpō,
- Hapkido,
- Kajukenbo,
- Kung Fu San Soo,
- Capoeira and various other styles.

Such experiences and education led Sifu Nick into teaching Jeet Kune Do for several years allowing him to fuel his desire to work with both his passion for film as well as martial arts. After attending school with a Major in Acting, Sifu Nick continued diligence and hard work to become a well-known professional Stunt Director, Stunt Performer, Fight Choreographer, Stunt Coordinator, and Second Unit Director. Sifu Nick is well respected and sought after within the film industry.

One night while waiting for a response to work on a new film, Sifu Nick came across an ad that Sifu Edward had posted to learn how to fight with a light saber. Of course, being a Star Wars fan, Sifu Nick had to check it out. From there, Sifu Nick's journey as a Saber Samurai had begun.

As for my journey? From a young age I have always had an entrepreneur spirit with skills of leadership and creativity. As I grew older, being successful in the business world was an inevitable outcome. While also helping several associates to grow their business, most of my work was done sitting behind a desk creating marketing campaigns, websites, and new ideas to increase public awareness. Unfortunately, this sedentary lifestyle produced almost no physical exercise and my daily diet had become a myriad of unhealthy foods that caused great stress on my physical health.

Soon I found myself in the hospital unable to walk due to the strain on my spine from excessive weight gain. Knowing that immediate changes in my life had to be made, I educated myself utilizing the health and fitness guidance of my closest friends and confidants.

This advice included an exercise routine that I had quickly admitted was both boring and tedious. This is about the time when a friend had introduced me to a whole new world that revolved around physical activities using light sabers. From there a new journey had begun. Soon I found myself achieving the cardio exercise, resistance training, and toning needed for a full body workout, all while having an amazing amount of fun with a light saber.

This is where my Saber Samurai journey began. Believing strongly in the "Henry Ford Approach" of surrounding yourself with the people who have the required skill set to get specific tasks done successfully... I purchased a European Franchise system that taught the sport of Light Saber engagements. It wasn't long after that when I became a Certified Instructor of the first two forms of Lightsaber Dueling within this European Light Saber Franchise System. Thus, using their Franchise systems alongside my own personal business knowledge and experience, within the first six months, I had grown the largest Light Saber Dueling Academy in the United States within this particular European Light Saber franchise organization.

After remaining with the franchise system for two successful years, I realized that internal changes needed to be made in order for light saber activities to reach their fullest potential within the United States. Remaining within that particular franchise model would not allow for these changes to happen. So with the help and alliance of the aforementioned Founding Masters (again the Henry Ford approach) all of whom shared the same visions, Saberation was born. A National Light Saber Martial Arts, Fitness and Athletic Association that not only focuses on the disciplines of Martial Arts, but the fitness and athletic aspect as well.

CHAPTER 2
Your Journey As A Saber Samurai:

Allow me to provide you with a little insight into the Saberation Empire and how through Saberation came the birth of other light saber industries and their strategic partnerships.

The following is a short list of the strategic partnerships we work closely with and will prove to be invaluable resources for you during your Saber Samurai journey.:

- **The Saber Life Community** (https://TheSaberLife.com) is our next generation social community for all light saber enthusiast.
- **Light Sword Martial Arts** (https://LightSwordMartialArts.com)is the world's first fully accredited lights sword martial arts academy.
- **Imperial Sabers** (https://ImperialSabers.com /)is our pro shop. A lot of our students and our clients go there to gear up and buy their light sabers, helmets, gloves and other items available in the Imperial sabers pro shop.
- **Build-A-Saber**, (https://Build-A-Saber.com/)where you can actually receive your light saber kit and build your own light saber from scratch.
- **Virtual Saber Academy**, (https://VirtualSaberAcademy.com/) learn the techniques of Light Sword Martial Arts at home
- **Total Saber Fit**, (https://TotalSaberFit.com/) the world's first 30 minute full body cardio workout utilizing the light saber.
- **Online Saberfit Bootcamp** (https://SaberFitBootcamp.com/)individualized fitness and health plan that allows a person to take advantage of the Total Saber Fit program from the comfort and privacy of their own home.

Hopefully by now you realize that when I share with you the various ways you can start a new career as a Saber Samurai, it's not about going out there to sell SAS. You're actually going out there to make a difference in people's lives. And we are going to arm you with the tools you need to be successful.

At this point I want you to sit there for a moment and consider what thoughts you had when you first saw the cover of this book. Did you say to yourself, Hmm, I can actually swing light sabers all day long and make really, really good income? Were you placing yourself in that picture, at that moment? What type of people did you see yourself training? Where did you envision yourself doing something like light sword martial arts? Or, did you envision yourself doing something like, Total Saber Fit?

So, why the light saber? Why do you think they are so enthralling? The light saber is actually one thing that spans generations with a unifying factor. Allow me to explain. In our academy we start training people as young as the age of eight and our oldest current student is 70years old. She actually attends with her daughter and her granddaughter. All three of them come to our dojo and train with light sabers.

Light sabers transcend generational boundaries and borders. Allowing people to come together because of their common interest. We have discovered that even people who classify themselves as introverts and passive in nature are instantly ready to attack or hit something the moment they put that lightsaber in their hand and they hit that ignition switch to light it up. It's an awesome sight to behold.

Another curious observation we have experienced is that there are three predominant categories of people that wanted to come in and swing that lightsaber. First were the competitive personalities. They wanted to fight and be the best. These personality types prove to be very interested in our light sword martial arts program.

Next are the people that realized very quickly how much they were sweating. They realized that they were getting a good workout. Looking at their health tracker stating something like, "oh my God, I burnt 1,000 calories in the last 60 minutes." Most of the time they didn't even realize just how much physical activity they were actually doing because they were so busy laughing and having fun. For those of you who actually go to the gym, how many times do you walk in and see a crowd of people that are actually laughing, joking, having fun, talking about gaming and all the things they did the night before? You don't usually see that in a fitness gym.

The third category of personality that enjoys our services are the people who just want to have fun. Sometimes people just want to laugh and experience something new and adventurous. These desires are definitely fulfilled when swinging a light saber.

So now the "Elephant In The Room". Let's discuss if there is really a need. This is a question that comes up quite often. Do people need lightsabers? The answer to that question is "YES"

! This is one of the most disturbing things I would like to discuss regarding "Living The Saber Life" and actually having and building a profitable career with a light saber.

Did you know that 25% (one out of every four) kids report being a victim of violent bullying? 65% of teens in the US have tried illegal drugs. You can actually Google these numbers. 78% of children with low self-esteem, engage in drugs, smoking, or self harm. 81% of teens don't get enough aerobic activity.

Now Let's talk about the adults here for a second. 80% of employees say they regularly feel stressed at their jobs. 68% of adults ages 18 or older are considered to be overweight or obese. 81% of adults don't get enough, weekly aerobic or strength exercise. 26% of all deaths are directly related to heart disease and lack of physical activity. Are you starting to see the pattern?

69% of kids under 18 spend more than five hours per day looking at their screens. ie. their mobile devices or computers. 69% under the age of 18. That's almost an eight hour workday. 48% of adults in the US have cardiovascular disease. The number one cause of death. 79% of parents wished that they could spend higher quality time with their families.

So let's discuss why we just went through all those facts and figures. When we say that you can actually have a profitable career as a Saber Samurai and that light sabers actually do make a difference in other people's lives: This is an understatement. We truly do make an impact and a difference in people's lives. When we first started offering Light Sword Martial Arts to the community and parents started bringing their children to us, I cannot tell you how many times these parents sat there in amazement because their child was actually doing physical activity. Their children were sweating their butt off, running around having fun swinging their light sabers. For many of these children we provide the only physical activity that they have all week.

For whatever reason, many schools apparently no longer offer Physical Ed (PE), or they don't have any after school activities.

Many children simply come home, get on the computer and you don't see them again until dinnertime. Then they disappear again right after dinner. However, with Light Sword Martial Arts, swinging a light saber became the highlight of their week.

We also serve a lot of military personnel. It is extremely common that when they come into our dojo after a stressful day at work, they walk out after their Light Sword Martial Art training session with their stress relieved. You can visually see that they're happy and they're smiling ear to ear ready to take on the rest of their day or the next.

Now here is something that happened totally unexpected on multiple occasions. This is something I myself cannot explain, but it happens. I had a couple students explain to me what Asperger Syndrome is. It was not a term that I had ever heard of before. I didn't understand what it meant to "be on the spectrum". or what this really was. So a couple of my students had actually sat down with me and they spent about two hours educating me on what all of this really was about. I was completely taken by surprise with this exposure to a whole new world I did not know even existed.

Come to find out the reason that they were telling me this was because I actually had several students in my dojo that had Aspergers at the time. I had no idea. I just knew that their training technique was a little different, but as it turns out, these particular students happen to be some of the most precise when it came to executing light saber training techniques. Many times I was left standing there observing in complete admiration. It was just amazing to see.

I remember when a parent came to me before departing for our National Tournament in New York. We were preparing to travel by van when she came to me and pulled me outside. She just started crying. I asked what was going on? Her son was going with us to compete in the National Light Saber Sport Competition. She went on to share with me that this was the first time he had ever gone anywhere without her or the family. Not only was he not afraid, but he was eager to go and didn't even want her around. This was "his" thing. The tribe that we had built were his family, his extended family. His confidence level and his ability to operate independently were visibly heightened. She just wanted to thank us. Those tears were tears of joy.

We wouldn't have been able to reach him in such a way without using the light saber. Yet he wasn't the only one. We later discovered that there were multiple students that were somewhere on the spectrum, or were highly functioning, but for whatever reason were drawn to the light saber. The attention that they placed on wielding it, the light. the sound, the personal development that came about.

I'm not a doctor. I don't presume to know anything about psychology or anything that's involved with autism, but I can tell you what I've seen with my own eyes and what I've experienced. This is what I mean when I used to have this phrase that I'd say, "like sabers are life savers' because whether it's social, emotional, mental or physical, there are so many wonderful benefits that come with physical light saber activities.

The strongest benefit of all perhaps occurs within the community you create. Wielding a light saber inside of a community you create provides a new type of bonding with people. You establish a sense of friendship as your social sphere and influence naturally expand. Plus you are providing everyone with exciting physical activity. So why not be the hero? Why not help solve the problems within your community and get paid to do it? You can actually be the one to step in and contribute something positive to your community that they would love you and embrace you for. Plus, it's not like you would be competing against thousands of people. Most likely you'll be one of the first in your community to be able to share this experience with other people.

CHAPTER 3

What About Those Walls?

Some of the walls that people have built during past conversations about becoming a Saber Samurai include...

- I want to enjoy life making money with light sabers, but I don't know how. I don't know what to do.
- I'm not trained or certified to teach anyone to use a light saber.
- I don't have the capital to open an academy or purchase equipment.
- I don't know where to find clients.
- Who's willing to pay me to teach?
- Exactly what am I even teaching or instructing them to do?

These are but a few of the walls I see built be people who want to live "The Saber Life" but allow fear and doubt to settle in. These are the reasons why we created a training program and certification program. Success as a Saber Samurai is not that difficult. You just have to care. If you have compassion for other people, then you have accomplished the biggest part.   Being able to wield the light saber happens in gradient stages.

What shines through and what people gravitate to, the benefits that people are receiving from what you are offering is rooted in your personal compassion for the betterment, happiness and health of others. People can sense and feel that right away.

If you are thinking that you don't have the capital to open a light saber academy or purchase light saber equipment, don't worry. I will provide you with solutions. I did not write this book to pitch you some $50,000 sales pitch to buy our franchise. That's not how this works. This is not how you become a Saber Samurai.

You may also be questioning where to find clients and who's willing to pay you to become their instructor? What am I even teaching or instructing them on? Again I urge you to stop worrying. In this book I will expose the solutions required to bring down those walls of doubt and fear. Throughout this book we will dive into your passions and strengths. as we build upon the mindset required to move forward in confidence.

When it comes to knowing where to find clients as a Saber Samurai, we have an entire blueprint and system to assist you with this. You are literally surrounded by hundreds of people, if not thousands of people right now that are willing to pay you to teach or instruct them to wield a light saber. Whether it be for fitness, for fun, competitiveness or just pure entertainment.

Often people just want something fun to do. They have nowhere to go. They want to spend some time with their family. They are looking for adventure and you would be the person able to provide them with that activity. Wielding light sabers expands across all generations. Mom, Dad, Son, Grandmother, Grandson, Cousin, Uncle, Aunt, all of them, all laughing, all enjoying themselves, all grateful that you are there to provide that opportunity for them.

"But Sifu", you might be saying, "I don't know how to market or even have a website, or contracts, or systems..." Fret not my young apprentice. I will not allow you to fall into a tank filled with sharks. When I first started in this industry, I started under a completely different organization. It was an Italy based company who had just expanded into the United States. They were more of a light saber sport franchise. When Sigu Julliana and I purchased their franchise and started building the business within months we became the largest, fastest growing light saber organization in the country within this Italian Franchise Organisation. As mentioned in Chapter 1 within our Bio, our success with this Light Saber Franchise was due to our vast business experience.

Sifu Julliana and I have owned and operated various businesses from restaurants, nightclubs, tax preparation agencies, fully licensed insurance agencies and more. We embraced all of those experiences, the good, the bad, and the ugly of business. Despite it all, there are just certain fundamentals of business that are just fundamental. We applied these fundamental principles to the light saber industry.

There was no manual for us to follow. We literally had to "write the book". Think about it. Where else can you currently go to learn the complete requirements and experiences required to establish a successful and profitable career as a Saber Samurai? If you decide that you want to open up, a restaurant right. Somewhere there is a course for that. There is a convention somewhere to address this topic. There's something somewhere that will instruct you on how to write the business plan or whatever you need to do to open this restaurant. Where to go get the equipment and the supplies, how to hire your staff for back house and front house operations. All of this has been mapped out. The same can be said for just about any other business out there. It's all been mapped out. However, where are you going to go to get the information to open a light saber academy? Where are you going to find that operations manual and policy directives?

Well, the good news is that's where we come in. We've done it. We do it. We've built it. We've had everything from city contracts to military contracts, to online operations, to offline operations. We have multiple instructors. We've built it from the ground up utilizing some of the most successful business practices combined from all the other industries that we've been in. Then we just applied those same principles here, including becoming an accredited martial art.

Another "Brick In The Wall" could be you saying…"I work another job. When, when will I have time to do this?" Well, we are not expecting or advising you to go out there and quit your job. First you should build your rapport within the community. Believe it or not, it doesn't take that long to accomplish.

Take a moment to think about the life you live in right now. If someone found out that you were out there wielding a light saber and teaching people how to do it, how long would you say it would take to spread from just word of mouth alone? How long do you think it would take for everyone in the area to know that this is what you do? In this book I will show you how to make being a "Saber Samurai" fit within your current lifestyle. If you choose to do this full time, I will show you how to scale it. But first we will focus on making it additional income. Then you'll understand how to make it your dominant income.

So why would anyone pay you to teach them light saber wielding? Because as a Saber Samurai you become the light saber expert in your community. How many light saber experts do you currently have making a difference in your community right now? How many people in your community right now are teaching other people how to wield their light sabers with fun and engaging activities? You probably do not have many to count right now, correct? In this book I will show you how to be the expert and understand all aspects of being a Saber Samurai.

I have had people say to me, "Sifu, I'm not in the best shape. How can I keep up with my own students?" Many want to be teachers or instructors and their primary concern is that they sometimes feel that physically they just can't get out there and swing that saber with their students for three or five hours. I hear things like…"you know, my knees aren't what they used to be." or "my back isn't what it used to be." I understand how some may feel. This is why I created an entire plug and play system for Saber Samurai which I will go into greater detail later on in this book

Imagine being able to build a career as a Saber Samurai so that you know every month you have created an additional income with consistent measurable growth. Imagine being able to build a business that thrives even when we have a crisis. Earlier in this book I wrote that we are an accredited martial academy, right. Did you know that during this past pandemic, we have seen so many martial art academies close their doors forever. Some of them have been there for 20 years or more, and they couldn't make it through the pandemic. They were destroyed. However, not only were we able to make it through the pandemic, we were able to continue to build upon our services offered. We were able to continue to expand. We were able to continue to offer the experience of wielding a light saber to people both nationally and internationally. The contents of this book will soon reveal how you can do the same thing.

Imagine consistent cash flow that did not start from zero every month. Often I have conversations with Millennials and with what is now referred to as Generation Z. Many of them have this idea that "you gotta be out there and you gotta hustle". My question is when has hustling ever been sustainable? Hustling Isn't something that's going to keep generating revenue for you month after month. I don't understand this ideology of "hustling". I like the idea of being able to provide a service to people that they actually want and are willing to compensate you for month in and month out consistently on a scalable level. To me, that just makes more sense.

If you've been searching for an opportunity that provides this positive ROI return on investment, you may have been trying real estate investment or playing the stock market, or you've been learning how to leverage cryptocurrencies. Yet you still haven't found something that's consistently lucrative. I can tell you right now, we've been doing this since 2018. Every year our Saber Samurai business keeps getting stronger. It's consistent and it's scalable. We don't have to keep looking for other opportunities. As a Saber Samurai we have found that greater purpose that actually allows us to get paid for creating a positive influence within our community.

I am not a fan of sitting at a desk or working on an assembly line for the rest of my life. I am not looking to sit at home watching life pass by either. My desire is to go out and make a difference in society. A positive difference with a light saber. So I'm going to have that time of my life. Remember at the beginning of this book I wrote how much I love my life? I do. I swear. I love my life. I literally wield a light saber. and I know I'm making a difference.

Are you financially set with your job but you feel like you are drowning in that box? There were many times in my past when I felt like this. When we had the restaurant it was actually on the beach. Do you realize the whole time we owned that restaurant that was on the beach (literally when you walked out the back door you were standing on the beach sand) I think I went to the actual beach twice. The whole time we owned that restaurant on the beach. I was working the entire time and the two times I went to the actual beach itself, my wife had to make me go.

When we owned the insurance agency and the tax preparation agency, I was head of marketing. As I was sitting at this desk in the company I actually co-owned with my wife, I still felt like I wasn't fulfilling my purpose. I remember asking myself, "is this what I was born for?"

Well, I had finally discovered my purpose the moment I embraced a light saber. When it comes down to seeing the expression on people's face when they ignite a light saber up for the first time. Think about when you lit up your first light saber, Think about the very first time you held your light saber and you hit the ignition switch and that thing lit up, just think about the expression on your face.

Now think about the expression on the face of a friend or a family member, somebody, when you put a light saber in their hand and they turned it on. Now imagine experiencing that from other people every day, all day. This is what I'm talking about.

So regarding all of these things that you're questioning and just not sure if you can do it, or if you're able to do it, it's not your fault that you have these questions or doubts, right? Because so many of us have been told things like, "stop dreaming".

Do any of these comments sound familiar?...

- Dreams, don't pay the bills.
- Go get a real job,
- Come back to reality.
- You got a champagne taste on a Kool-Aid budget.

Well to all the naysayers I say this…. Just remember, everything that exists in reality was first formed and
thought. Period!   Everything that currently exists in reality right now was first formed in thought.

Dreams + Action= Reality.

If somebody thought about any electronic device you're using right now and "NOt" done anything to build it, you wouldn't own it today. Someone has to think about it, act upon it and then produce it. This is exactly how Saberation was born. We thought about it. We created it, we produced it. Then once we produced it, we said, "you know what? Let's train other people and show them how they can do the same thing."

Another topic of concern for many people is exactly how much should they charge for their light saber services as a Certified Saber Samurai? How do I make six figures a year? One of the topics that will be discussed in this book is called Operation Plugin. This is where I will share with you exactly how we get students, how much we charge, how we actually locate them. The truth is that you don't need a large audience. You don't need a big team and you don't need to have mastered marketing to create this profitable and purposeful life as a Saber Samurai

CHAPTER 4
Operation Plug-In

Sifu Julliana and I were working with an Italy based Light Saber Sport Franchise Organization when we established the largest, fastest growing light saber academy within this particular franchise organization here in the US. The secret to our success is what this chapter is dedicated to because we still implement. and apply the tenets of this secret I'm about to share with you to this very day. This secret still contributes to our continued growth and stability. It goes by the name of Operation Plug-In.

Operation Plug-In is very significant with regards to the results it yields? So what exactly is Operation Plug-In? Our objective was to launch a national marketing campaign that would create a large scale awareness of who we are and what we do to initiate a massive wave of new academies. We wanted to expand our academy and create more academies. We wanted to fully utilize our local, existing students that we trained to become Saber Samurai. The goal was to create a condition that allowed us to be able to better utilize them. Afterall, what good is training people to become Saber Samurai If they are just sitting there twiddling their thumbs because they have nothing to do, nowhere to go, no one to train and no nowhere to make a difference?

Such a situation would leave us not really accomplishing anything. We wanted to be able to utilize the sSaber Samurais that we raise up and dispatch them into the community. In addition, we needed a way to implement a training program that would effectively and consistently produce high quality Saber Samurais that we could deploy nationwide. This is the primary objective of Operation Plug-In.

Let's discuss why we called it Operation Plug-In. The reason is very simple. If you have a rechargeable light saber, what do you do when the battery dies? Plug it in. What do you do when you need to get access to abundant quantities of something like power? You need to plug in. So when I sat down and I thought about this it became obvious that when the light saber gets low on energy, when it gets low on resources, when it's about to die or we need it to last longer or be more powerful, we have to plug it into a power source. When we started our academies, our journey, our path towards becoming a Saber Samurai, we started with zero students. We had no one to teach? So how do we get an abundance of something we need, we need to plug in to who or whatever has that source in abundance.

It is important to really look at why I use electricity as an example here. When you plug into an outlet, you have to make sure that it is compatible. That voltage has to be compatible. Otherwise you're going to blow a circuit. If you plug your light saber into a high voltage outlet, what's going to happen to the motherboard? It will be destroyed. Your light saber will become a shelf ornament. Well, the same thing happens when you are looking at expanding your private practice as a Saber Samurai. You don't want to just go out and approach everyone. You want to plug into a group or an organization or something that is compatible with your beliefs, your skillset, your interest level, your ability to communicate with.

HOME SCHOOL COMMUNITIES

Communication is essential. You want to make sure that you are able to communicate with who and whatever it is that you are planning on plugging into. So one of the first sources we attempted to plug-in to was Homeschool co-ops. Currently many of the homeschool community in the US are diligently seeking new, innovative, exciting activities to introduce to their children while maintaining their individuality and the core values of the group as a whole. One thing that I have come to realize when dealing with the homeschool community is that they are a very close knit community. One of the reasons the parents are homeschooling is because they want to preserve their core sets of values and beliefs, while educating their children. Homeschool communities tend to constantly be in need of PE (Physical Education) and the ability for the kids to be able to go someplace to have physical activity and be able to interact with like-minded peers that share the same core values.

When you go onto, for example, Facebook, start researching groups for homeschool and local homeschool organizations. Let's say you live in Atlanta for example. You type on Facebook search, Atlanta homeschool groups, or if you live in Los Angeles, you put in, LA homeschool. You'll find all of your local homeschool groups will start to populate. So who are in these groups? The parents, right? The parents are in these groups communicating to other parents. We merely contacted the moderator or the owner of these homeschool groups. We introduced ourselves through a private message, or a direct message. AWe let them know what our intentions are and explain how we are offering light sword martial arts or light saber classes to provide physical activity and entertainment to all who participate. A We go on to extend our offer to this group and even create a special group day and time for each individual group. So let's say you had "Group A", on Mondays at two o'clock, I would host a special session for "Group A" and I'll even have special prices just for homeschoolers. So let's say(as an example only) you normally charge $50 per student per class. So for homeschoolers, you would then turn around and say, well, we'll give you a discount and we'll charge you $30 per student per class. This way the homeschoolers appreciate the fact that you are giving them a discount. Many times when you're dealing with homeschool households, you have a situation where there's one parent that's working and one parent staying home with a child. So any type of financial consideration is greatly embraced.

End result is that there's a need being filled. You are providing:
- physical education and physical activity for the children,
- a place for them to come together and socialize and have activity.
- You're giving them consideration and showing financial preferential treatment there.

As you look up homeschools in your local area, and you look at the number of members that are in those groups, you have some groups that are 3, 4, 500 members deep. You have some group that are three, four, 5,000 members deep, and they are all, if you put in the right keywords, local to your community and all people that you can serve immediately. So how much did you have to pay to market yourself to them? Answer: $0.

PUBLIC SCHOOLS AND COLLEGE CAMPUSES

Next we focus on local public schools and college campuses. Typically a school has a student activity coordinator. That's what they call them here in Virginia. In other States, they may have different titles. They may call them guidance counselors. Basically, it's the person who's responsible for implementing activities within the school that the students participate in. What's their job? Their job is to determine what physical activities will be offered to the students this year? What kind of after school activities are they going to offer? What type of sports are they going to offer? Are we going to do a school dance this year?

There is a student activities coordinator who works at each school and that's their responsibility. So we start training at the age of eight. Some of you may be gifted enough to where you can work with the younger. I recommend no younger than the age of eight. Because if you are actually trying to teach them something and have them retain it, then eight seems to be about as young as you want to go. When you go younger than that, most of the time, I'm not saying 100% of the time, but most of the time when they're younger than eight, then you just have kids running around hitting any and everything. They're not really paying attention to anything you're trying to teach them.

Whereas we have observed that once children turn eight years old there is a tendency to start comprehending the techniques better. So when you're dealing with the school system, keep that in mind. Middle schools and High Schools have a great need for a variety of activities due to the mindset of our youth during that age. If you can meet with a Student Activity Coordinator and say, "Hello, I have this wonderful program where we provide light sword training using a light saber. The students are provided great physical activity while engaging in competitive team and group activities." This is the type of verbiage that I recommend you use. Do not approach them with statements like, " yeah, we're going to be hitting the heck outta each other with light sabers!" Keep in mind that whether you approach elementary, middle or high school, take a moment to realize just how many potential students are in each school. I mean, we're talking thousands per school.

Then there's the college campuses. Remember that everything I am sharing with you here are also techniques and methods that I have personally used myself. I'm not sharing theory here. I am sharing with you things that we have successfully done. Here in Virginia at a college named Old Dominion University (ODU) we actually founded an Official Chartered Student Light Saber Club. This was a student-run organization endorsed by one of the professors at the university. In order for this to happen a professor has to be willing to Sponsor the Club. That means that they'll be responsible for whatever that club does. Then the students have to come up with a charter. They have to elect their Board of directors and then establish their bylaws and operating procedures.

After the club becomes officially endorsed on the college campus, then the college students will go out amongst their peers on the campus and start recruiting other students to become a part of their club. This is where you want to make sure your pricing is appropriate for the students. There is a whole methodology that goes into that.

COMIC-CONS

ComicCon networks are like " fish in a barrel." I really get excited talking about the ComicCon because wow, man, we go to these ComicCon and we literally will walk away with 300 or more people who want us to contact them to schedule a Demo Session. We've gone to ComicCon and we've walked away with so many leads that it took us weeks to get through them all. keep in mind that you can either attend a ComicCon, as a vendor, which requires a small amount of upfront capital to cover the booth fees. That's basically your cost. You don't have to worry about your marketing or anything like that because whoever's hosting the ComicCon is the one that covers the additional expenses.

All you have to do is be there with your literature. We typically do a light saber giveaway. using a raffle of some sort. We simply announce that we're going to give away a free light saber at our tablet there and we have them enter their information into our online entry form to win. Now all of their contact information was just digitally placed into our database and we can follow up with them later and offer them a free two week training session. They then come out to our academy and once they start, they realize how much they love it, and then next thing we know, they sign up to become students because of the amount of fun they are experiencing.

There is an entire system to this, but just keep in mind what your initial investment was. The cost of the booth and a light saber to give away. That was it.

We literally filled our classes doing these comic cons time and time again. We've even hosted our first ComicCon for the first time in 2019 in Virginia. We called it Saber-Con. The entire event took place inside a local shopping mall where we were also launching the Grand Opening of one our newest locations inside the very same mall. It was glorious.

CHARITY AFFILIATIONS

Charity Light Saber Sport Competitions. This is a great way to get exposure. Here's what we did. We hosted a charity event. Remember earlier I mentioned that some of my students had educated me about autism and Asperger? After sitting down with them for over two hours I decided to do a charity. fundraiser. We decided to raise money and donate it back to organizations established to help families support their children or other family members living with the condition of autism.

I decided to host a charity light saber competition. We rented a sports facility that we could use for onsite training classes. During the competition we spent a little time training the participants on how to duel using a few basic moves. Then we actually, after we trained everyone on the rules of engagement and what was considered legal vs. illegal in the competition. Finally, we cut 'em loose on each other.

Because it was a charity competition we even had sponsors who provided tax exempt donations to the cause. There were also vendors who came in and set up their booth with items to sell. The best part was that they paid for their vendor space. This helped to offset the cost of the rental of the sports facility.

The whole time of the event we were able to promote our academy and our classes. So while people were coming by checking things out and participating, we were letting people know, we do classes here locally. The next thing you know, people were signing up for a demo class.

So why do I do demo classes? Very simple. If you say, I want to go into a basketball camp or I want to go take basketball classes, you know what that is. If you say soccer, you know what that is. The same with football and baseball. Everybody knows what these activities are about. However, you say, "I want to go take a light saber class." People look at you in an interesting way. Thinking, "what the heck are you talking about?" So you have to offer a free demo session in order to introduce people to what it is. Giving them an opportunity to fall in love with it.

So we did this charity and then we took the proceeds and donated it to a tax exempt nonprofit organization who then dispersed it to the intended recipients. It was an awesome event. With regards to the community, we became very well known, very fast.

GOVERNMENT CONTRACTS

Government contracts for us are special classes with special discounts for City and government workers. Some of the most stressful jobs out there are jobs where you are working for the government or municipalities? One opportunity to plug-in would consist of offering team building events exclusively for . city and State workers, Designate one night per week and announce to the various City and State offices that you want to work with that is they show up and present their credentials then come in and participate in some fun light saber team building activities. Maybe even get the Boss.

RWhat you will find is that coworkers will start coming in and having a great time together. This became very popular for us even in the private sector. We had people from large health insurance organizations coming in for team building activities. We had people from a large graphic design company. We just had so much fun with all of them. Especially when they got to beat up their boss, I mean, it was just ridiculously fun.

We currently have a contract with Langley Air Force Base, and Fort Eustis Army Base. Both are located here in Virginia. There are so many benefits to working with military families. We learned this firsthand. We service airmen,sailors and soldiers coming home from deployment. Many are looking for activities to do as a family. Our classes serve as a means to reintroduce family a sense of bonding. It is heart wrenching to know the sacrifices that a lot of the military personnel make in order to protect our country. A lot of our military are deployed for two months, four months, six months, a year, two years. AWhen they come home to their families and their household, sometimes they feel like complete strangers. So they look for activities that they can do as a family where they can have fun and get to know and be with each other. In this sense, light saber activities became a therapeutic service that we could offer. Our students come in, they learn a new skill and then we always spar at the end increasing our level of fun even more.

I remember when we also had the opportunity to provide demo classes to two separate platoons. It was a huge training session, I think we had about 40 airmen there that we had to train all at the same time. We trained them all how to do the light saber basic combat maneuvers and then we let them spar each other. You could definitely tell, they were rival platoons in a competitive way.

Then at the end there was this grudge match between the two colonels. All I could do was stand there in silence and stay out of their way. There was definitely something going on there… and they needed to "grudge it out". But honestly it was a lot of fun.

We still work with Langley Air Force Base. One perk of working with the military is the fact that they do a lot of events all year round. Some are open to the public and some are open to just military personnel and their families. Yet because we have contracts with them, we are often invited to many of these events.

There are also a lot of benefits to working with civil service. Often there is a friendly local rivalry between the police department and the fire department. So when you actually plug that in with the fundraising that I mentioned earlier, and offer a fundraising light saber competition between the local police department versus the fire department. Oh my, just in the community alone, I mean, they're going to tell everybody and they're going to brag and they're going to boast about how they're going to whoop each other's butt. Yet it's all good, wholesome fun for everyone.

To be able to organize a fire department versus the police department light saber battle where all you have to do is set it up an entry fee and provide both teams adequate training sessions (equal time). For example, you can offer four classes before the event. Make it mandatory that each participant attends a minimum of four training sessions. Then during those four classes you can teach them the basic maneuvers in order to compete. This way everyone will be utilizing it and applying the same techniques.

There is a gold mine with regards to introducing yourself to the community.

SUMMER CAMPS

Summer Camps can be a fiercely competitive market depending on how large of an area you live in. But many times when you start looking for summer camps, there is not a shortage of options. However, what there is a shortage of are unique activities. So instead of hosting a summer camp perhaps consider plugging- in to a summer camp and offer your expertise with that summer camp. Simply introduce yourself and mention that you provide light saber sporting activities. You could also say light saber physical activities, depending on if you target the competitive side or the fitness side. This is in reference to the three personality categories I mentioned earlier.

Essentially you have competitive, fitness and entertaining personalities. Depending which of those three areas you target, it will determine which approach to use. The entertaining part would probably resonate with the summer camp, as well as the fitness part and the competitive market. Actually all three would resonate with the summer camp. That's one of the unique ones. On this option you would just offer your services for a flat fee. Don't try to do a per person charge on this one. You would simply say, " I'll come and provide these light saber training sessions for one week for a flat fee of X amount of dollars. So you show up to a summer camp, you teach for a couple hours and you go home and you just made really good money.

FITNESS GYM ALLIANCES

The fitness industry is one of the reasons why we created Total Saber Fit. When considering the typical fitness gym, how many gyms do you know of where you can walk in and see people are in there working out, laughing, joking, having fun, while genuinely just so happy to be there? All while maintaining an entire community feeling. How many gyms do that versus people that are kinda in their own little world, they are not paying attention to anything or anyone else.

I feel surrounded by all these people when I go into a typical gym and I think to myself "I get outta here." So when we designed the Total Saber Fit workout, we did it so that it would be interactive with laughter and fun. People are goofing off and having fun with each other, but they're still burning calories. They're still sweating.

When you look at a fitness gym, you can look at this from two different ways. You can look at this from a mom and pop fitness gym, or you can look at this from a fitness trainer perspective. Both have the same problem of saturation. With fitness trainers, you can throw a rock 50 feet in any direction and probably hit one. There's an abundance of fitness trainers. There is an abundance of fitness gyms. While everyone is trying to figure out how to get people to sign up for a whole year for only 20 bucks. You know, that's how bad it has become.

So this is when you can go to either a fitness trainer or a mom and pop, I'm not talking about a large franchise chain, I'm talking about your local mom and pop fitness gyms. and you say, "I'm going to provide you with the chance to offer light saber fitness classes. We have a 30 minute Cardio program called Saber Jam. It's like Zumba with a lightsaber. Just swing the light saber with our personal trainer and you got the music going and everybody's just having fun." Then let them know that you will offer these light saber fitness classes for 30 minutes and only charge " X" amount of dollars per person. Or, can offer to split the revenue entirely.   You will be the only game in town offering these light saber fitness classes.

The fitness trainers and mom and pop fitness gyms will all love you because you would have helped solve a problem for them. You would be flooding their gym with all these people cause they're coming for the light sabers.

So I want you to take a moment right now to think of at least two methods that would serve as good options within your community.   How can you apply at least two of these options in your community in a way which also makes you feel happy and fulfilled as well?

CHAPTER 5:

Branding Yourself As A Saber Samurai

Let's talk about "you" as a brand. Branding yourself as an industry expert. Undoubtedly you will need to be branded as the local Saber Samurai authority. As we further discuss how to do this, keep in mind, I'm only going to share with you the actions that we ourselves have done. I'm not going to share with you theory, ideas, concepts or possibilities. We know what works because we have a proven model of success for it.

I recently saw a commercial that was talking about leaders and how they don't have the luxury necessarily of always following "the path". How often they have to be pioneers and they have to be the one creating the path for others to follow. As a Saber Samurai, that's exactly what you're doing. You are creating a path for others to follow after you. Where else are people going to turn for reference on being a successful Saber Samurai in their community? Or receiving the services of a local Saber Samurai? It should be you. You should be that local authority available to help the community.

I am sure that you probably already know 2, 3, 4 people of whom if you were to approach them and ask, "Hey, how would you like to make a living? A very good living, wielding the light saber every day?" would respond with a "heck yeah!" So when they say, "heck yeah, I want to do that" what do you do next? Who are you going to be for them? Where are you going to guide them? What are you going to do to help position them, to help you build your personal empire and help them build their personal empire?

One way to build your personal brand is through alliances. Surround yourself with the very essence in life you want to inherit, or the very people in life you would like to emulate. Such as other authorities in other areas of life that are a compliment to your own desires. How do you become an authority? By surrounding yourself with authorities. Birds of a feather, fly together. Ever hear that saying?

My wife and I had a truly revealing moment some years back as we were taking a personal inventory of our life. I love sharing this story. This is a very dear story to me because it was a major turning point for me and it truly helped to change the entire direction that my life was heading. Okay, so we were sitting there in our house staring at one of my dry erase boards as we discussed the fact that we were working ridiculous hours every day. I mean, we're talking about 14 to 16 hours workdays. Yet financially at the time we were still struggling. We were self-employed. So we asked ourselves how is this even possible? How can you work so hard for so many hours and not have the financial rewards of your labor? We just couldn't understand this.

So I got on the dry erase board and I drew two lines going from top to bottom. This created three columns. At the top of the first column I wrote, "People we communicate with daily." I then proceeded to list every person that I talked to, that we both had talked to on a consistent daily basis. There were at least 30 people on that list. In other words, the phone was constantly glued to our ear. We thought we were moving and shaking. Just remember that just, because you're out doing a lot, doesn't mean you're getting a lot done. Keep that in mind.

In the second column I listed what we wanted to accomplish in our personal lives. We had to "be real" with ourselves and discuss what were our true goals? What were our aspirations? Why were we doing what we do on a daily basis? What was the purpose? So we wrote down our dreams and the things that we were actually working towards. We listed our aspirations. The infamous "this is what we're doing this for" list.

Then in column three we wrote down all the names from column one that were helping us accomplish all the goals listed in column two. So if you were in column one and you were contributing to our goals in life in column two, we wrote your name in column three.

Out of the 30 or more names in column one... 5 of them made it to column three. Five! Which means we were communicating with 25 or more people per day that were consuming our time and offered absolutely no contribution towards our personal goals in life.

Once we realized this, we were able to immediately disconnect from the madness. I looked at my wife and said, "look, these communication lines are not contributing to our life at all. These lines are not contributing to our goals. These communication lines are acting as siphons and they're siphoning out our time that we can never get back." At that moment we made a decision to disconnect ourselves from the other 25 people on that list that were consuming time and our life energy. We then decided to only communicate with the people that were actually contributing towards our personal goals in life.

From that moment forward we were able to spend more time being laser focused on our personal goals and actually accomplish them. During this process we learned to surround ourselves with the people that are successfully where we want to be and are successfully doing what we want to do. People that actually are authorities in their field. Now I'm not saying to go find a bunch of people that are authority in the SabLight Saber industry. Currently that will be very challenging to do because you are going to become that person yourself. However, you want to find people that are authorities in their particular fields and learn their success habits.

So the first thing you want to do is make alliances. The next thing that you want to do is join business associations. Support your local civic groups or associations. You don't have to go out and join every organization out there. Sometimes they just want your support and encouragement. There's plenty of networking opportunities. Especially as a Saber Samurai. Realize that when you walk into any type of business setting, and all of a sudden you whip out a light saber. The first urge people will instantly experience is to hold it and take selfies. So now you have all these professional business people walking around the room with light sabers, and what's the first thing people want to do when they get a light saber in their hand? Hit somebody! I mean, it's crazy. It just immediately turned into an exciting environment filled with smiles and laughter.

I remember a time when I was negotiating with a city organization, a particular city organization. And I had my PowerPoint presentation discussing the benefits of being able to provide life saber activities as an add-on service to various city programs. I had this whole professional presentation mapped out and I was ready to roll.

As I gave my spiel and the two ladies that were sitting there listening to me and watching my presentation. They were responding with the typical, "yes. Okay. Yes Mr. Armstrong, that's great. That's wonderful. Yes." It didn't take much to realize that I had lost their interest. They were there in the room with me but they were not hearing me. That's when I remembered the most important part of the meeting. The whole reason I was able to book the appointment in the first place. The "Real" star of the show. Nobody cared really about the words that I was speaking at that time, the star of the show was the light saber. The reason that they booked the appointment with me in the first place was because the proposal was to discuss lightsabers and that's what they wanted to see. So I asked. "would you like to see a light saber? Would you like to hold one?"

They both looked at each other and shouted "Yes!" Be right back, I said as I ran outta their office, down the hall, into the parking lot and to my car. I just so happened to be traveling with quite a few light sabers. So I grabbed a couple light sabers and I ran back into their office where we were meeting and I gave it to them. Instantly they perked up as they grabbed ahold of the hilts. "oh my gosh, this is... these are awesome!" Well you know, I said. It gets better. Just hit the button right there. As they hit the button located on the hilt the light sabers immediately ignited and you just saw both the blade and their faces light up at the same time. Then you know what happened next. They start hitting each other.

A bit nervous, I point out that the office is a little small. I didn't want them to break their computers. So within the blink of an eye the two of them were out in the hall sparring each other. Pretend like they're fighting in some epic galactic battle scene. Then they start running in and out of the offices of their coworkers. You see them running into this one office and then you hear someone scream, "what the..." , then they run into another office. Looking at me, one of them says, "Don't go anywhere." then they both run right past me disappearing behind a set double doors. Closing the door behind them, again I hear screams of "What... No way!... What in the..."

Both of the young ladies come from behind the double doors, closing the doors behind them. They were laughing their butts off. Apparently what was going on behind those double doors was an actual board meeting.   Their bosses and other managers of the city were all having a meeting. They literally barged into that meeting with two light sabers and commenced hitting these people. Then they ran out of the meeting laughing. Before you ask, yes, they did keep their jobs.

It is just amazing to witness how presenting these light sabers before people can inspire such joy, happiness and laughter. Seeing the internal youth spring up from the very essence of a person's soul. These are the types of experience that, as a Saber Samurai, you are bringing to the world.

Another part of your Branding process will include media and public events. We had to learn how to communicate with the local media and how to host events that draw out the media's attention. Seldom will you find yourself in a very strong or advantageous position if you're continuously running behind the press begging for their attention. However, if you create an event that draws their attention, then they become the one seeking you out for an interview.

For example, we have a local radio station, FM 99. They have a local beauty pageant that they do every year called Rock Girl.

Locally it's a really big deal. Many of the local ladies compete to become the Rock Girl for the year. There's photo shoots and news media everywhere. The winner is announced during a big annual concert with national top of the chart bands performing.

One year we decided to become a sponsor to the Pageant. One of the sponsor benefits included the radio station coming out to our location to host the tryouts. During the photo shoot and tryout we had t photos of all the female contestants holding the light saber as part of their glamor shot. Which by the way was plastered all over social media and became viral. Also as one of the sponsors the radio station was also pushing these photos and our company to their entire listening base. And I think this particular radio station might have been around for over 50 years. They have a very large listener base and marketing list. This was a beautiful opportunity for us and definitely positioned us as a strong authority with regards to our Brand.

Take some time to give consideration towards what two options you can apply to establish, solidify and build your brand and position yourself as the local authority. The Saber Samurai is known for bringing joy, happiness and laughter into the community as well as provide physical benefits through the use of light saber during physical activities. How can you become that person or that Brand that people think of and call?

CHAPTER 6

Establishing Your Audience

Step one of establishing and building your audience is to identify yourself.   We need to know who, what, when, why and how. For example, when you Google our Brand "Saberation" you will immediately see that we own our name and our identity. When people receive business cards or brochures from us or see our sponsored ads or anything that we may do; Brand the name Saberation.

When you Google "Saberation" there is no question as to who we are, what we do, where we're located. We make it very obvious as to exactly when we do things, why we do what we do and how we do what we do. We own all our identity. That is always step number one when you go out into the community and you start introducing yourself and you are positioning yourself to become that authority, as we discussed in the previous chapter, one of the primary actions that people will take is to Google you. If you are a true authority in your industry or your niche, then you should not be a mystery when people start researching you.

As a Saber Samurai I need to know that you know who I am and what a Saber Samurai is. We are introducing ourselves into people's lives and injecting ourselves into their personal space. We are becoming a part of their personal association. They're bringing us into their sphere. Some are introducing us to their children. They are introducing us to their wives and their husbands. They are trusting that we are credible and trustworthy.

In order for them to get this sense of trustworthiness from us, it is our obligation and our duty to identify ourselves. If somebody came to your house and rang your doorbell, you opened the door, they proceeded to just walk in, you've never seen this person before and they didn't even tell you who they were. What would you do? I want you to think about that for a moment, because essentially we're asking people to let us into their home or let us into their lives. We're asking them to embrace us yet and they don't know anything about us. They don't know who we are. They don't know what we do other than the fact that we have light sabers. They don't know where we're located. If something occurs and someone want to find out more details about your light saber program, do we have any listing anywhere? Could they find out when you're available? For example, are you available on Sundays at 6:00 PM? Are you available on Saturday mornings at 10? Does anyone know your story and why you decided to become a Saber Samurai? These are important factors to take into consideration.

Who exactly would become a Saber Samurai? Why would anyone do that? Typically, most people will not even understand how you do it. How are you qualified to do what you do? What makes you a Saber Samurai? So, step one, we need to identify who we are. Take a closer look at our Brand. When you type in Saberation into Google, you know who we are. Type in the words "Light Sword Martial Arts" into

Google. You know who we are. Type in the words "Total Saber Fit". You know who we are. When you type in "Imperial savers", you know who we are. That is step one. Identify yourself.

Step two is to duplicate yourself. All right, after you have identified yourself, the who, what, where, when, why and how, right now you want to duplicate that self because people may not be typing in your name in Google. They may be typing in your name on Facebook. They may be typing in your name on Twitter. They may be typing in your name on Instagram. So when they're typing in your name, in all these different places to find out who you are, what is your identity? Are you there to be found? Google, believe it or not is not the end all be all. It's still very powerful. Don't get me wrong. However, in today's society, more and more people before they go to Google, are going to YouTube trying to do their search because they don't feel like reading. They want to watch a video. I've seen this. I've done this. People are using other platforms to find out more about people's identity. So step number two, duplicate yourself and make sure that your identity is provided on multiple platforms. Not just one.

Then there is step number three, introduce yourself. When we came into this industry and started living the Saber Life, when we made a decision to become Saber Samurai, the very first thing we did that created a major win for us is step three. We introduced ourselves. We use the site called "Meetup". This site is a sleeping giant. When we first started I said to my wife, "we need to start teaching classes." At that time, our finances were wrapped up into our other business ventures. And honestly, I really didn't know how to do sponsored ads on Facebook and all that stuff.

Traditional marketing was hefty financial commitment. Radio ads, television ads, newspaper ads, all of them. I was trying to find a solution to get in front of the most people without it costing me an arm and a leg, where I could build an audience quickly. In the previous chapters I discussed going out and building alliances and talking to organizations all of which really work. I've done it. It works. It works awesomely. I mean, it really works a lot, but still, it takes a little bit of time. It takes a little time to get on the phone, set the appointments, go out there and talk to the people and close the deal. Right?

Even after building the alliances and everyone's on the same page, you still have to schedule the event. Or, you have to plug into an event which is on a scheduled day or time. None of these things just happen overnight. There's no button that you push, no magic bullet. That is it. It takes cultivation and vision. You have to be focused. All of these things are prerequisites to building this empire.

However, due to the situation that I was facing at the time, I needed to start a class and generate additional income. I needed to make money and I needed to prove that this was a viable business venture. I needed to prove it now, not later. So we stumbled across this site called "meetup". What meetup essentially is, if you're not familiar with it, it's a social platform, but it is a platform designed to group people that have similar interests so that they can go out and meet up in certain locations to partake in such interest together. Its a great way to make new friends that have similar interests.

Let's say you have a group of people who love horseback riding. They formed their own little group on meetup. They all joined this group for horseback riding, and guess what? They all meet up next Saturday. to go horseback riding together. If you have a group that loves painting. Guess what? Next Monday, they all meet over this location and they go paint together. Some groups may love book clubs. They like reading. Some groups may love wine tasting. That's very popular on the site. So they'll meet up and they'll go wine tasting together. Some people like bowling, archery, paintballing, anime, board games. I mean, there's all kind of interest in meetup, including light saber enthusiasts! People that are star war fans, or that just love light sabers.

The beautiful part about this is this site is nationwide. And the popularity of this site is greatly anchored to demographics of the area in which you live. So someone who lives in Los Angeles are going to have a whole lot more meetups available than someone that lives in rural Nebraska. It is based on the people in that area with common interest coming together and doing the activities. However, what I didn't know about meetup, and this is why it became a wonderful secret weapon for us, is that when you joined meetup and you put in your interests, or you put in what you're doing, the website itself works off of keywords you place within your event and your profile. They work off of a tag system. So if you put in that you are starting a new group and they say, okay, what is your group about? You think, oh, well, my group is about light sabers and star wars. It's about the empire, whatever you want to say.

As soon as you create the group, meetup turns around and notifies everyone in their network, in your area that has said, they're interested in these types of activities and immediately notifies all of them about your new group. Normally you have to pay big bucks for that type of announcement. Meetup. does it as part of their platform. It's built in and it's amazing.

So here's what happened. We were renting a place by the hour in an indoor sports arena. We secured the venue for three hours so we could do a two hour event. But we needed a half hour for setup and a half hour for breakdown. We then started a new group on meetup and announced that "we're a light saber group introducing light saber combat classes to the community. Come on and hang out with us. This is a free vent. We just want you to come hop, hang out with us, have some fun with us. We're going to provide the light sabers, all you have to do is come help us with the fun."

We had somewhere between 10 or 15 people that said, "heck yeah, I'll be there!" They all showed up. We're talking about people that are gamers. military personnel, you know, family members looking for a fun experience, all of them showed up. It was a beautiful, beautiful thing. We taught an introductory class and showed them what we're all about. We had fun with them and we spared each of them individually. That free event of 10 to 15 people converted into 8 new students who paid and signed up for a class on the spot. A two hour free event netted us more than the average person makes during two hours of work at their job. Do you understand the power of this? We continue to use meetup even to this day

I wanted to share that with you because it is so powerful to understand. If you're going to be the authority in your area you cannot forget to

- Step one, identify yourself, let people know who, what, where, when, why and how.
- Step two, duplicate yourself. You have to get on multiple platforms. Everyone doesn't just use Google alone. They use other platforms as well, mastering the identity and then duplicating that identity and then introduce yourself.

- Then you do step three. Would you like to take a few moments to talk to me some more about this? Would you like to get to know me? I'm hosting a free net? Would you like to come? Right? Here's your invitation? No strings attached. Just come have some fun with me.

That was the start of our empire. Those eight people. That was the start. Next thing you know, those eight people went out and told all of their friends. Remember I said, some of them were gamers. What do you think they talked about when they got back on to play their game? That's right. The light saber class.

CHAPTER 7:

Living The Saber Life

As Saber Samurai we are the pioneers of this new and exciting industry. But how does one actually become a Saber Samurai? How do we learn and teach the techniques of being a Saber Samurai? This happens to be one of our specialties.   This is what we do.

We train people to become Saber Samurai. We train people to become appreciative of the art itself. Even if they decide not to go out and teach it. Our entire foundation, our entire business model is bringing on students and training them in the ways of the S.A.B.E.R.   So the next question is how?

How do we negotiate the terms of Operation Plug-In? Between the homeschooling co-ops network, college campuses, the comic cons, the government contracts, military contracts, civil servants. What are the terms that you're going to negotiate? What's the pricing model? Where do you even start with regards to pricing?   What are the legalities involved?

How do we structure the training curriculum for the students? So you go out there and you get, let's say, 10 people that raise their hands and they say, "okay, I want in, I want to do this light saber training." So you say, "okay, well, we're going to start class next week."   What's the curriculum? Where do you start?

How do you set up the membership website to take the payments? So not only are we talking about the curriculum of what to teach, how to teach when to teach it, but how you're going to get paid? Are you going to have people just whip out their wallets and give you cash, or are you going to have them whip out their credit card. How are you going to accept the credit card payments? Is this going to be a monthly charge? Is it going to be a weekly charge? Is it going to be a daily charge? Is there going to be a free trial involved? How are you going to set up these payments so that that money gets into your bank account? That's what we're talking about, right? How to earn that extra income wielding a light saber.

What about automations? How are we going to automate the establishing of your identity, duplicating yourself and introducing yourself, everything we went over in the previous chapter? I realize you may have another job you currently work. You have additional things that you need to do, at certain points in time during the day or during the week. I mean, who really wants to sit at the computer and read every Facebook comment that comes in or every Instagram comment and respond to everyone that comes in with questions. If you try to do all this while at work, you probably won't have that job very long? But if you don't respond, then the people begin to feel like, "oh, well, no one there to listen to me." So we need to automate this. We put all this effort and energy into making our presence known. In today's society we must have these social media accounts set up and we have these Google listing accounts set up and we have all these press releases going out and the phone starts ringing, wait a minute, what phone? We'll get to that in a minute. But the phone starts ringing. People start leaving voicemails. They start sending emails, they start sending text messages and they're saying, Hey, this guy's so awesome. can you come to my Cub scout organization? or can you come to our church youth group and do something, can you come to our office and do team building with all my staff? Meanwhile, who's responding? Who has the answers to respond with If you're not the one answering?

Remember in a previous chapter I stated that you should surround yourself with the very things in life you want to become. You should surround yourself with other authorities. I sincerely hope that by now I have proven myself to indeed be an authority in this industry. All of the "hows" that we just went through are the very things that we ourselves had to answer. We had to provide the answers to those questions. We had to create the answers to those questions because prior to us, the answers did not exist. I'm not trying to be vain in any sense of the word, if you don't, believe me, try Googling it and finding the answers on your own.

We had to create the answers. Therefore, being an authority in this industry, I think we have something of value that we can possibly offer to you. You don't have to reinvent the wheel. You did not start reading this book to create more work for yourself, or to create a bigger headache or stress for yourself. You don't have to do that. We've already taken care of you. We have your back. We've already had it set up. We have pioneered, established, grown, profited it from and now, (drum roll) We have figured out a way to duplicate our success.

How do I learn the techniques of being a saber samurai in the first place? The answer: Light Sword, Martial Arts: Virtual Saber Academy, 2.0. Please note, we didn't decide to just grab some light sabers and practice different forms of martial arts using light saber instead of a sword. That's not how Light Sword Martial Arts was born. Now I know that there are some other martial arts academies out there who may do other types of swordsmanship where instead of using an actual sword, they replace the weapon with the light saber, but we didn't do that.

We actually had to adapt the martial art to the weapon. We had to adapt the martial art to the tool because when you're utilizing a steel sword, there's a cutting edge and there's a non cutting edge. Sometimes there's two cutting edges, depending on the type of sword. Sometimes the handle is flat. Sometimes the handle is round. My point is the weapon of choice determines the form being used. There's certain techniques that you're not going to do with a one edge blade that you would do with a two edge blade. So it's not as simple as just replacing the weapon. We literally had to reconstruct the techniques so that it was beneficial to an actual light sword or light saber.

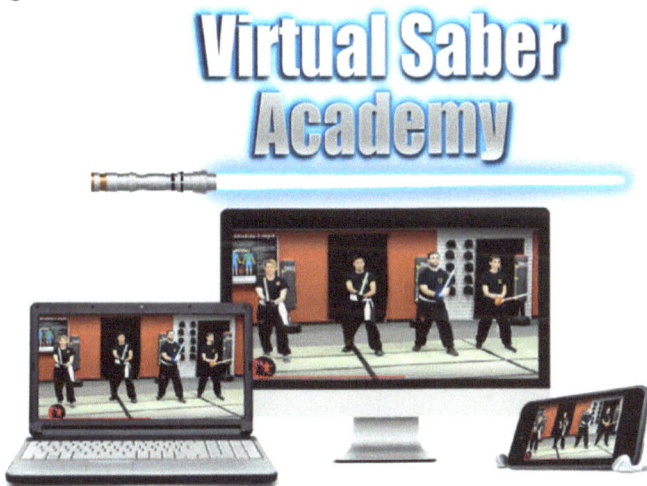

You can discover more by visiting
https://VirtualSaberAcademy.com

Next topic of concern is how to negotiate the terms of Operation Plug-In? How do I negotiate the terms of homeschool co-ops networks, college campuses, public school systems, ComicCon networks, charity affiliate, uh, affiliate go contracts, military contracts, civil servant plans, summer camps, fitness. What do I say? How do I charge? What do I do?   The answer in our new system.

- All of our contract templates,
- Membership agreement templates
- Profit & Loss Excel sheets and more

We put everything into a turnkey system for you. Remember in today's time it's all about automations. Our goal was to automate as much as possible for you, making sure that you can duplicate what we do and get the same result or greater that we get. So we have thrown in our contracts. We've thrown in the templates that we actually use. You can access our membership agreements and discover how we charge? Why we charge the rates that we do charge and when do we charge them?

What about how to structure the training curriculum for your students? Guess what. We have a Saber Samurai Curriculum done for you. Discover exactly what to teach each day? How and when to move on from one lesson to the next? What are you looking for to verify that your students have actually gotten the technique that you're trying to teach? What are some of the key components that they need to understand from day one so that your students always leave your class with the same amount of limbs that they walk into your class with?

Want camps? ok We'll give you camps. If you want to do a light saber training camp, you will need the curriculum for that. What about how to structure the camps? Is it going to be a full day camp? Is it going to be a half day camp? Is it going to be a one week camp or a two week camp? What are you going to do during these times? What do the kids need to bring? What do the parents need to know? How do you want to price these things out? How much staff are you going to need? What about the medical requirements? You know. Don't worry. We have a system for that too.

And then there were the Demo Sessions. Remember when I mentioned in the previous chapters about doing introductory demo sessions free of charge just to get people in the door. Remember that first one I did with, with meetup? It was a free demo and we spent two hours with them. Then next thing you know, at the end of those two hours, I had eight people sign up on the spot and my first class was created. Well, what exactly did I do during those two hours? That's part of the curriculum that's included in the Saber Samurai curriculum.

What about setting up memberships and taking payments? Imagine people yelling, "Hey, just take my money! Give me a light saber and take my money! Let's go have some fun!" Well, how are you going to do that? How are you going to set up and coordinate the student rooster and memberships? You guessed it, We created a Saber Samurai Academy Software to do everything for you.

Remember? I said, we have to duplicate what we do. That was our goal. After we pioneer it and we expand it and we profit from it, then we have to duplicate it. So we've done it for you. So you also can access your very own Custom Saber Samurai Software and Mobile App. Yep, the mobile app is included with the software and the mobile app also handles all of your online retail

Custom website? Coming right up! Remember we talked about making yourself known, okay, what are you going to do about the website? What are you going to list on these Google listings pages? And when you go to these social media profiles and they say, "OK, what's your website URL?" Where are you going to send people to check you out? We got you. We built it for you and built into it is also your billing and payment management system. You'll be able to send people a right to your website. They can put in their information and you'll be able to collect payments. You can even do monthly or weekly subscription payments. Whatever you want. It's easy to set up and easy to configure. And we walk you through it.

There are so many other features and benefits to our Saber Samurai Success System. Honestly I would have to add another chapter to this book to list them all.

To see view everything for yourself visit:
https://SaberSuccessSystem.com

CONCLUSION:

In conclusion, living The Saber Life as a Saber Samurai is both financially rewarding and emotionally fulfilling. I am so grateful and honored to live a life that I love, Surrounded by people I love and who love me as well. I look forward to the day when Saberation becomes a household name and being a Saber Samurai becomes one of the most sought after careers in existence.

Even if for some reason you decide that Becoming a Saber Samurai may not be right for you right at this moment, I encourage you to join us in our Private Network where you can meet and perhaps make new friends with other Saber Enthusiast such as yourself. Membership is FREE and there are no strings attached. Just a good community filled with good people who enjoy life and light sabers!

Come Live The Saber Life With Us!
https://TheSaberLife.com

www.ingramcontent.com/pod-product-compliance
Lightning Source LLC
Chambersburg PA
CBHW041005210326
41597CB00001B/21